# BEETHOVEN CLASSICS
## *for Easy Piano*

On the Cover:
*Village Landscape in Morning Light (The Lone Tree)* (1822)
by Caspar David Friedrich (1774–1840)

ISBN 978-1-5400-9068-3

Copyright © 2020 by HAL LEONARD LLC
International Copyright Secured   All Rights Reserved

For all works contained herein:
Unauthorized copying, arranging, adapting, recording, Internet posting, public performance,
or other distribution of the printed music in this publication is an infringement of copyright.
Infringers are liable under the law.

Visit Hal Leonard Online at
**www.halleonard.com**

Contact us:
**Hal Leonard**
7777 West Bluemound Road
Milwaukee, WI 53213
Email: info@halleonard.com

In Europe, contact:
**Hal Leonard Europe Limited**
42 Wigmore Street
Marylebone, London, W1U 2RN
Email: info@halleonardeurope.com

In Australia, contact:
**Hal Leonard Australia Pty. Ltd.**
4 Lentara Court
Cheltenham, Victoria, 3192 Australia
Email: info@halleonard.com.au

# Contents

# MINUET IN G MAJOR

By LUDWIG VAN BEETHOVEN

Copyright © 2014 by HAL LEONARD CORPORATION
International Copyright Secured   All Rights Reserved

# FÜR ELISE
## (For Elisa)

By LUDWIG VAN BEETHOVEN

Copyright © 2006 by HAL LEONARD CORPORATION
International Copyright Secured   All Rights Reserved

# "MOONLIGHT" SONATA
## (First Movement Theme)

By LUDWIG VAN BEETHOVEN

**Adagio sostenuto**

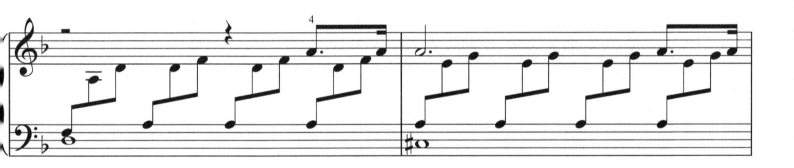

Copyright © 2020 by HAL LEONARD LLC
International Copyright Secured   All Rights Reserved

# ODE TO JOY
## from SYMPHONY NO. 9

By LUDWIG VAN BEETHOVEN

Copyright © 2020 by HAL LEONARD LLC
International Copyright Secured   All Rights Reserved

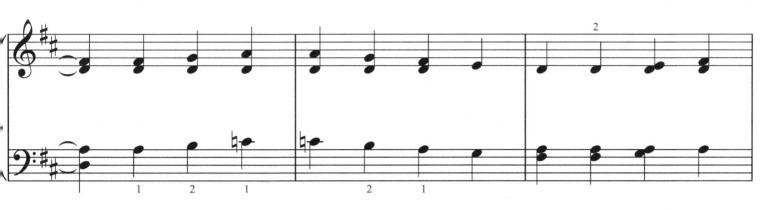

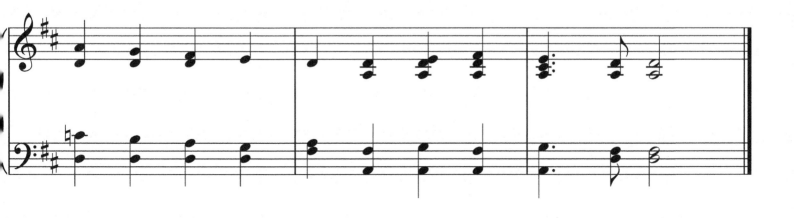

# OVERTURE TO EGMONT
## (Themes)

By LUDWIG VAN BEETHOVEN

**Allegro**

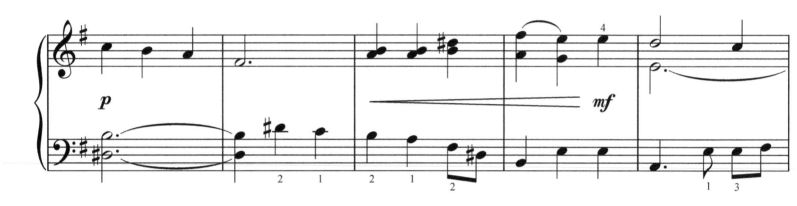

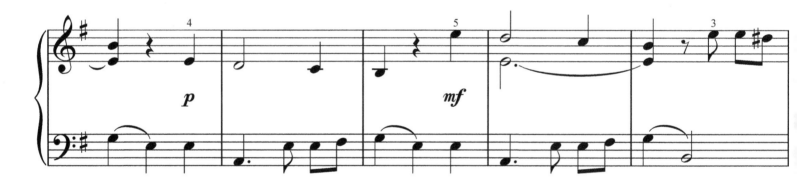

Copyright © 2020 by HAL LEONARD LLC
International Copyright Secured   All Rights Reserved

# "PATHÉTIQUE" SONATA
## (Second Movement Theme)

By LUDWIG VAN BEETHOVEN

**Adagio cantabile**

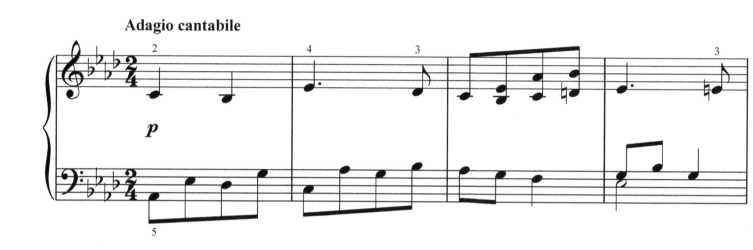

Copyright © 2020 by HAL LEONARD LLC
International Copyright Secured   All Rights Reserved

# SYMPHONY NO. 1
### (Second Movement Theme)

By LUDWIG VAN BEETHOVEN

**Andante cantabile con moto**

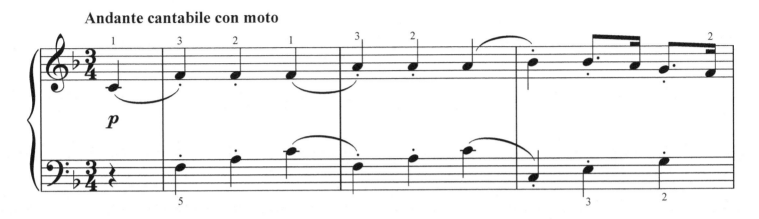

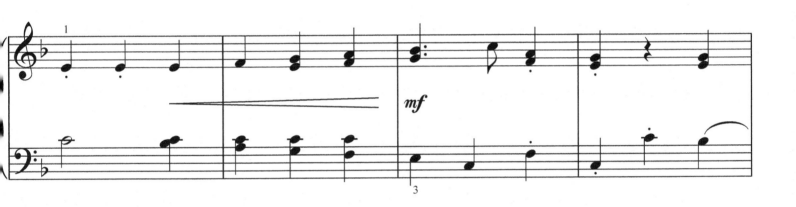

Copyright © 2020 by HAL LEONARD LLC
International Copyright Secured   All Rights Reserved

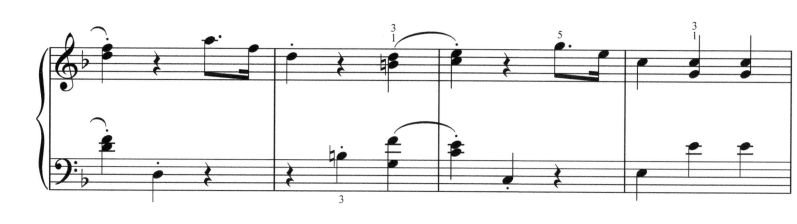

# SYMPHONY NO. 1
### (Third Movement Theme)

By LUDWIG VAN BEETHOVEN

**Allegro molto e vivace**

Copyright © 2020 by HAL LEONARD LLC
International Copyright Secured   All Rights Reserved

# SYMPHONY NO. 2
## (Third Movement Theme)

By LUDWIG VAN BEETHOVEN

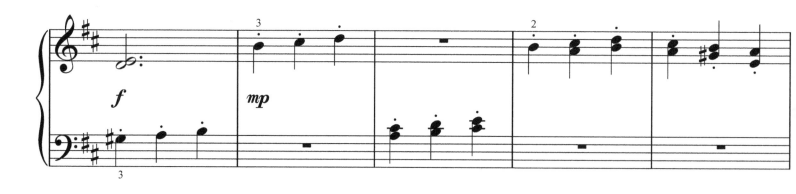

Copyright © 2020 by HAL LEONARD LLC
International Copyright Secured   All Rights Reserved

# SYMPHONY NO. 3
### (First Movement Theme)

By LUDWIG VAN BEETHOVEN

**Allegro con brio**

Copyright © 2020 by HAL LEONARD LLC
International Copyright Secured   All Rights Reserved

# SYMPHONY NO. 5
## (First Movement Theme)

By LUDWIG VAN BEETHOVEN

Copyright © 2020 by HAL LEONARD LLC
International Copyright Secured   All Rights Reserved

# SYMPHONY NO. 5
## (Second Movement Theme)

By LUDWIG VAN BEETHOVEN

Copyright © 2020 by HAL LEONARD LLC
International Copyright Secured   All Rights Reserved

# SYMPHONY NO. 5
## (Third Movement Theme)

By LUDWIG VAN BEETHOVEN

Copyright © 2020 by HAL LEONARD LLC
International Copyright Secured   All Rights Reserved

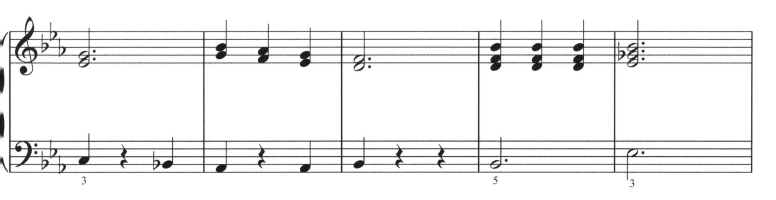

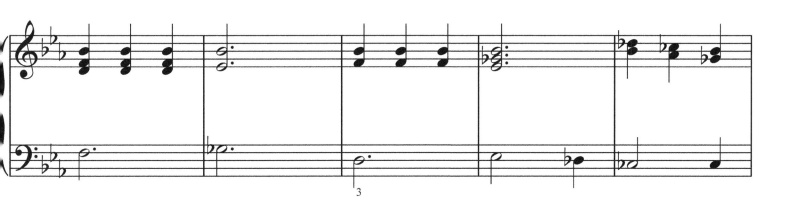

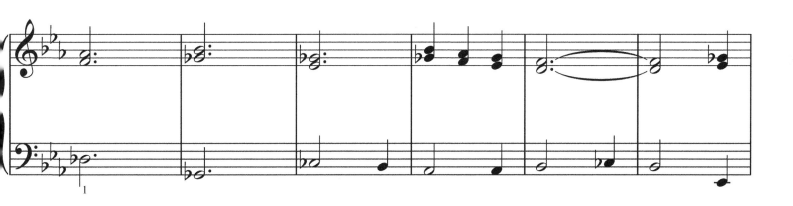

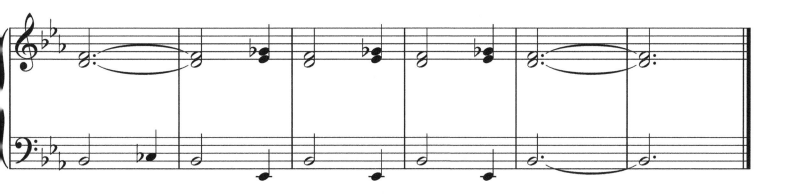

# SYMPHONY NO. 5
## (Fourth Movement Theme)

By LUDWIG VAN BEETHOVEN

Copyright © 2020 by HAL LEONARD LLC
International Copyright Secured   All Rights Reserved

# SYMPHONY NO. 6
## (First Movement Theme)

By LUDWIG VAN BEETHOVEN

**Allegro ma non troppo**

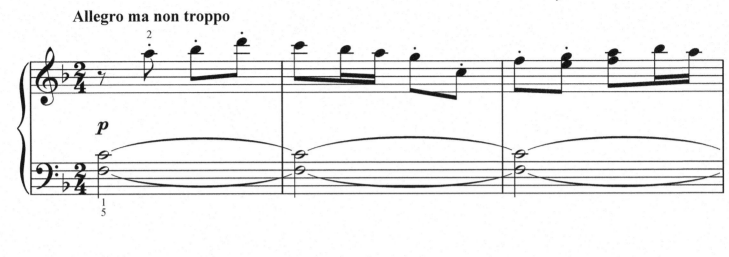

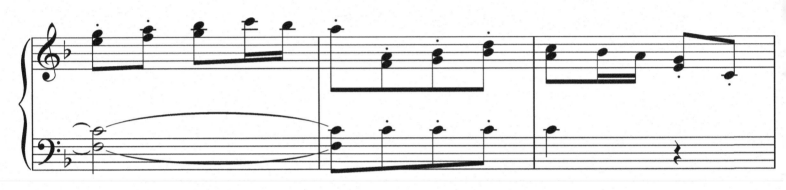

Copyright © 2020 by HAL LEONARD LLC
International Copyright Secured   All Rights Reserved

# SYMPHONY NO. 6
## (Third Movement Theme)

By LUDWIG VAN BEETHOVEN

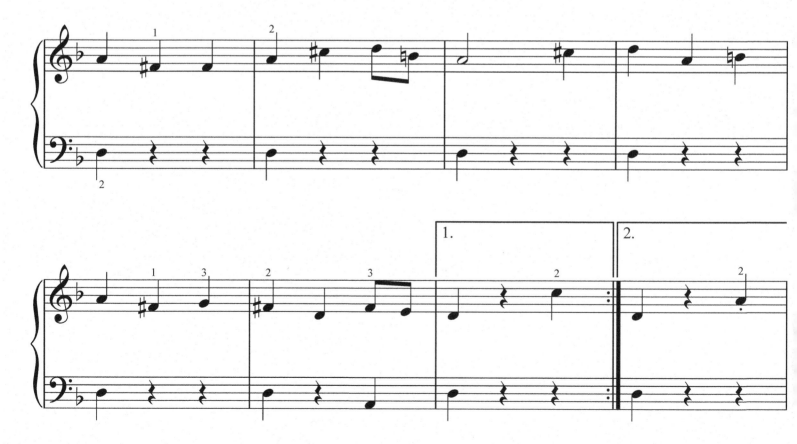

Copyright © 2020 by HAL LEONARD LLC
International Copyright Secured   All Rights Reserved

# WELLINGTON'S VICTORY
## (Themes)

By LUDWIG VAN BEETHOVEN

**Tempo di Marcia**
"Rule Britannia"

Copyright © 2001 by HAL LEONARD CORPORATION
International Copyright Secured   All Rights Reserved

**Tempo di Marcia**

"Marlborough"

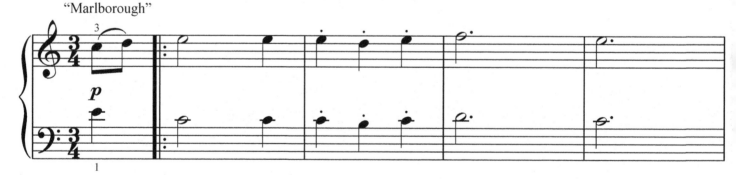

# SYMPHONY NO. 7
## (Second Movement Theme)

By LUDWIG VAN BEETHOVEN

**Allegretto**

Copyright © 2020 by HAL LEONARD LLC
International Copyright Secured   All Rights Reserved

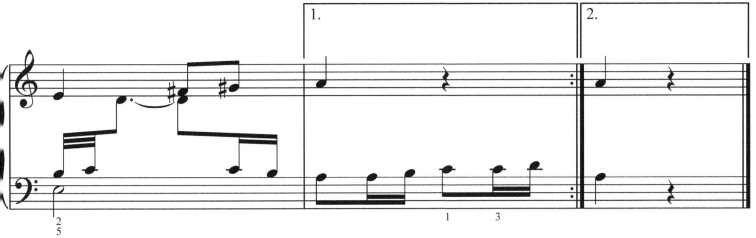

# TURKISH MARCH
## from THE RUINS OF ATHENS

By LUDWIG VAN BEETHOVEN

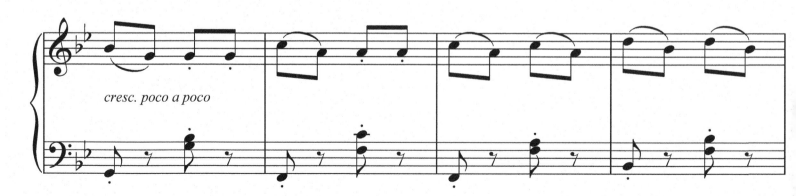

Copyright © 1999 by HAL LEONARD CORPORATION
International Copyright Secured   All Rights Reserved